Do-It-Yourself Ear Training

Written and narrated

by

RONALD HERDER

© 1983, 2000 Ekay Music, Inc.
333 Adams Street
Bedford Hills, NY 10507

About The Author

Author/composer Ronald Herder—former Editor-in-Chief of Associated Music Publishers and current Music Editor for Dover Publications, New York—has for over a decade been on the theory, composition and musical theater faculties of Manhattanville College and Purchase College (State University of New York). A graduate of the University of Pennsylvania, Miami University of Ohio, and Fontainebleau Conservatory, France, he has won France's *Maurice Ravel Prize in Composition*, Italy's *Concorso Internazionale*, and a composer's grant from the National Endowment for the Arts.

Herder's thirty-year involvement in creating practical, workable educational materials for beginners in music is highlighted by *Tonal/Atonal*—his widely read workbook in ear training for the modern student. Reviewers have praised its "revolutionary central theme" and called the course "...the most enlightened departure [in ear training] we have seen for many years."

Now, *Do-It-Yourself Ear Training*—narrated and performed by the author himself—joins Ron Herder's library of attractive, easy-going studies for learning musicians who seek genuine mastery in the shortest time and in the comfort of their own home.

to Ed Shanaphy,
publisher and editor-in-chief
of Sheet Music Magazine,
whose belief in new approaches to old ideas
made this publication possible.

INTRODUCTION

This is exactly the kind of information-packed, easy-going self-study music course we've always wanted to publish.

Back in the days when we started out as untrained musicians, we were hungry to find a way to learn as much as possible about music without the pressures and scheduling and cost of traditional schooling.

We wanted to be able to hear and understand rhythms, melody, and harmony... to be able to play and write down a tune we heard, or one we made up... to play better by ear... to get experience in transposing a piece from one key to another.

We wanted to understand what *really* went on in a piece of sheet music, and to know how to interpret those wonderful masses of music symbols.

If we had had a simple, enjoyable course like this one, musical life would have been a lot easier. Now that this one is in your hands, we are delighted for you.

Do-It-Yourself Ear Training is a step-by-step course that you can take at your own speed.

If you're a beginner who loves music and needs basic information, this course is for you. It starts with *basic* basics and supports you every step of the way with simple explanations, solid directions, and attractive examples to read, write, and play.

If you've already had some musical training, and just want to "fill in the gaps," this course is for you, too! All you need to do is move past any lesson that's too easy to one on exactly the level that works for you.

And even if you're a trained musician, or a professional performer, you'll welcome the chance to work with any or all of the *157* dictations in rhythm patterns, melodic intervals, and harmony.

In short, *Do-It-Yourself Ear Training* is a course for *everyone*, no matter which level you begin on.

The course covers an enormous amount of ground in the space of its five CD's: from the easiest traditional rhythm patterns to jazz syncopations... from basic intervals to complete melodies that you'll actually be able to hear and write down... from basic triads to the full, rich chords found in both pop and classical music.

Ron Herder is highly experienced in both the popular and classical worlds, and brings elements of both to this wonderful course: ragtime side by side with Brahms... folk music next to Chopin. He deals with music of *all* styles to illustrate his informal, entertaining, highly informative CD sessions.

And you use everything you learn as you move *at your own pace* through *four* sessions devoted to rhythm, *five* to melodic intervals, *four* that concentrate on harmony, and a special section that combines rhythm and melody in seventeen excerpts from folk, pop, and classical music.

There's no other course quite like it!

THE PUBLISHERS

BEST RESULTS

How To Use This Material

This CD/workbook program is designed for one purpose: to make you a better musician by giving you the practical means to hear more, to read faster, to be better at playing by ear, and to give you a working understanding of all the elements that are basic to music.

Very few musicians are born with a "good" ear. A good ear for rhythm, melody, and harmony is something we develop through training—a step-by-step process that we have to do every day, a bit at a time. Developing the ear is in fact like developing any set of muscles, or developing any set of learned responses. Right now you may be handling a job, driving a car, cooking a meal, running a household, playing your favorite sport,

playing an instrument—all, activities you learned step-by-step, mastering each part before you went on.

Sharpening your ear works exactly this way. In this course we'll work with small units, then go on to bigger and more challenging experiences. This necessary process requires your patience: Do a little work as often as you can, and enjoy each step along the road to complete mastery.

A self-study course means that you can work *at your own pace.* You can review any CD as often as you wish. You can listen to an explanation or music example repeatedly, until it becomes clear. There is no pressure and no competition; it is your course.

Some Practical Guidelines

Remember that all of our work is well within your reach. There are no tricks or mysteries to any of this. What you accomplish, and the amount of time you spend doing it, is entirely up to you.

You can go through this course in one of several ways:

The ideal way is to play the CD's while you are at your keyboard, with a pad of music paper at hand. This allows you to transfer what you hear or write directly to your instrument.

But this may be impractical. If you know that you will be working in a room *without* an instrument, buy an inexpensive paper or

plastic keyboard replica at your local music store, or design one yourself on a strip of cardboard. Then, as you play the CD, finger the model keyboard as though it were a real one. This will give you a way to associate what you hear and write with various finger positions on the keys.

As for playing the CD's while you are driving, this is a fine time to review material you've already studied. And it's a perfect opportunity to get the sounds into your ear: the pulsation of this or that rhythm pattern, the sound of an interval, the special color of a chord.

The Four-Step Method

Active Listening

For each music example you hear on the CD, try to focus *all* of your attention on the sound... *really* listen to it... get the feel of it in your ear: its special tone color or pulsation (whatever applies), perhaps something it reminds you of... anything that will help you register that particular sound as being special and unlike any other sound. This is *active* listening—the opposite of passive listening, hearing-without-hearing, or listening with self-defeating distractions.

From Sound to Touch

Transfer what you hear to your instrument. Touch the keyboard. Look at the keys. Watch how your fingers play. Away from your instrument, look at the keyboard diagrams in the workbook, imagine yourself playing the keys, or picture and "finger" an imaginary keyboard in your mind's eye.

From Sound and Touch to Written Notation

Translate both the sound you hear and your keyboard experience (real or imaginary) to music paper. Even the music paper, if necessary, can be imaginary: Imagine a music staff in your mind's eye, and notice how the notes are arranged in that mental picture.

Reviewing

Never hesitate to replay what you did not understand the first time. Explanations and music examples have different degrees of difficulty. Even the most experienced professionals replay, reread, rehearse. It is a natural part of the process. If something is not clear, *don't let it pass by.* You will need it to go on.

RH

CONTENTS

CD 1 / Track 1

RHYTHM PATTERNS

HOW TO DRAW NOTES Track 2

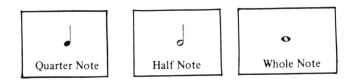

HOW TO MEASURE THE DURATION OF A NOTE

Each note has a specific *value,* or duration, that can be measured by comparing it to regular, evenly spaced pulsations called the *beat.* In popular music, the most common unit of measurement is the quarter note.

A SIMPLE QUARTER-NOTE BEAT Track 3

KEYBOARD DIAGRAM OF THE BASIC BLUES PHRASE Track 4

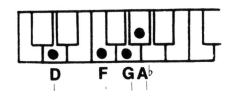

BASIC BLUES PHRASE (Staff Notation) Track 5

SAMPLE RHYTHM MODEL Track 6

THE TIME SIGNATURE

The *time signature* is a simple number formula consisting of two numbers. The *top* number indicates the *number* of beats in each bar. The *bottom* number indicates what *kind* of note represents the beat. In the time signature $\frac{4}{4}$, the bottom number *4* means that a *quarter note* represents the beat. In $\frac{4}{4}$, therefore, each bar will contain four quarter notes *or their equivalent*.

RHYTHM MODEL NO. 1

RHYTHM MODEL NO. 2

Track 7 *Dictation*

RHYTHM MODEL NO. 3 **Track 8**

THE DOTTED HALF NOTE

A dot after a note means "plus one-half" — that is, we extend the length of the note by adding on one-half of its original value.

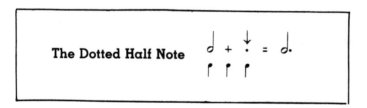

RHYTHM MODEL NO. 4

Track 9 *Dictation*

RHYTHM MODEL NO. 5 **Track 10**

Track 11 *Dictation*

THE REST: How to Notate Silence **Track 12**

Each unit of silence has its own symbol, called the *rest*. We can think of each kind of rest as the *silent* counterpart of each kind of note.

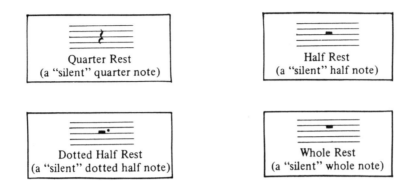

Quarter Rest
(a "silent" quarter note)

Half Rest
(a "silent" half note)

Dotted Half Rest
(a "silent" dotted half note)

Whole Rest
(a "silent" whole note)

RHYTHM MODEL NO. 6

*In a silent bar, the whole rest is placed in the *center*.

RHYTHM MODEL NO. 7

 **Track 13** *Dictation*

*In bar 1, the silence in the *middle* of the bar is usually notated as *two quarter rests*. Some composers prefer to substitute *one half rest*.

SLICING UP THE QUARTER NOTE **Track 14**

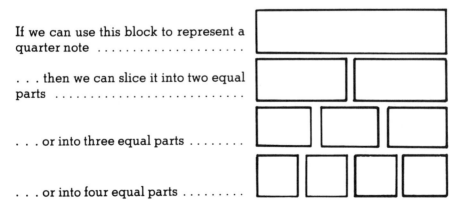

If we can use this block to represent a quarter note . . . .

. . . then we can slice it into two equal parts . . . .

. . . or into three equal parts . . . .

. . . or into four equal parts . . . .

ALL FOUR OF THESE POSSIBILITIES TAKE UP THE SAME AMOUNT OF SPACE.

Translated into musical notation, these blocks become:

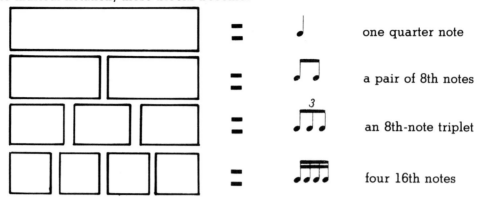

= ♩   one quarter note

= ♫   a pair of 8th notes

= ♪♪♪   an 8th-note triplet

= ♬   four 16th notes

ALL FOUR OF THESE POSSIBILITIES TAKE UP THE SAME AMOUNT OF **TIME.**

"A PLAY ON WORDS"

HOW TO DRAW THE EIGHTH NOTE **Track 15**

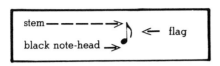 can also be written this way:

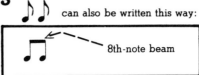

QUARTERS AND EIGHTHS

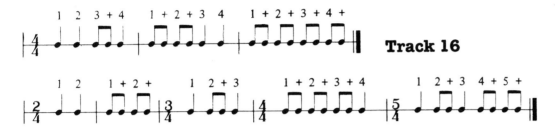 **Track 16**

HOW TO DRAW THE SIXTEENTH NOTE
Track 17

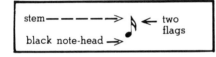 is usually written this way:

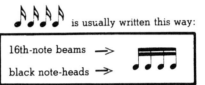

QUARTERS AND SIXTEENTHS

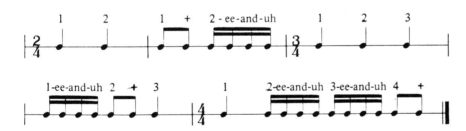

QUARTERS, EIGHTHS, AND SIXTEENTHS **Track 18**

HOW TO DRAW THE EIGHTH-NOTE TRIPLET **Track 19**

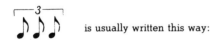 is usually written this way:

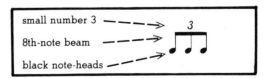

11

QUARTERS AND TRIPLETS

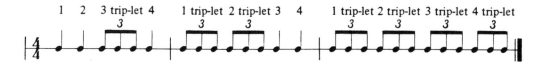

QUARTERS, EIGHTHS, TRIPLETS, AND SIXTEENTHS **Track 20**

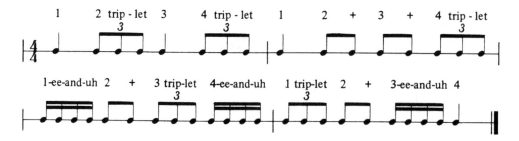

RHYTHM MODEL NO. 8 **Track 21**

RHYTHM MODEL NO. 9 **Track 22**

*In ¾, the half rest may be rewritten as *two quarter rests*.

**Although a silent bar in ¾ can be represented by a dotted half rest, it is traditional to use a *whole rest* — meaning "a whole bar" of silence.

Track 23 *Dictation*

SYNCOPATION **Track 24**

Syncopation is a shift of accent from a strong beat to a weak beat. We can also create a syncopated feeling by substituting *silence* for sound on a strong beat, or on a strong *part* of a beat, thereby weakening the strong-beat feeling.

RAGTIME PATTERN A-1

THE SIXTEENTH REST

Notice that both the 16th note and 16th rest have *two* "flags."

RAGTIME PATTERN A-2

SAMPLE FOR A ONE-LINE RHYTHMIC DICTATION Track 25

RAGTIME PATTERN A-3 Track 26

 **Track 27** *Dictation*

THE TIE

The tie — written ⌣ or ⌢ — ties together notes with the *same* pitch, making a longer sound. The duration of the tied notes equals their *combined* note values:

RAGTIME PATTERN B-1 Track 28

RAGTIME PATTERN B-2 Track 29

RAGTIME PATTERN B-3 Track 30

13

Track 31 *Dictation*

RAGTIME PATTERN C-1 **Track 32**

G A_ G_ C D E♭   F G_ F__ G G♯   A C_ C♯ D E   F

RAGTIME PATTERN C-2

RAGTIME PATTERN C-3

RAGTIME PATTERN C-4

RAGTIME PATTERN C-5

Track 33 *Dictation*

Note: The substitution of an 8th note for two tied 16ths is permissable *within* the beat (as shown in Patterns C-4 and C-5). It is incorrect, however, to apply the same substitution **if the tied notes belong to two different beats** (such as all of the ties between Beat 1 and Beat 2 in the examples above).

CD 2

RHYTHMIC VARIATIONS ON "SCARBOROUGH FAIR" **Track 1**

PITCHES AND RIGHT-HAND FINGERING FOR "SCARBOROUGH FAIR"

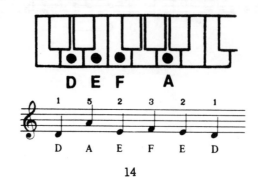

14

A You already know . . . that a beat can be represented by a quarter note. In this case, the bottom number of the time signature is always **4**.

New information: *Any* note value may represent the beat. If an *8th* note represents the beat, the bottom number of the time signature is **8** ($\frac{2}{8}$, $\frac{3}{8}$, $\frac{4}{8}$, etc.). If a *16th* note represents the beat, the bottom number of the time signature is **16** ($\frac{2}{16}$, $\frac{3}{16}$, $\frac{4}{16}$, etc.) If a *half* note represents the beat, the bottom number of the time signature is **2** ($\frac{2}{2}$, $\frac{3}{2}$, $\frac{4}{2}$, etc.).

RHYTHM MODEL "A"

Track 2 *Dictation*

Track 3

B You already know . . . that a quarter *rest* is a unit of silence that has the same value, or duration, as a quarter *note*. We can think of the quarter rest as a *silent* quarter note.

New information: The 8th *rest* is a unit of silence that has the same value, or duration, as an 8th *note.* We can think of the 8th rest as a *silent* 8th note.

Notice that both the 8th note and 8th rest have *one* "flag."

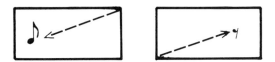

RHYTHM MODEL "B"

Track 4 *Dictation*

Track 5

C You already know . . . that a quarter note divides equally into two 8th notes.

New information: The 8th note divides equally into two 16th notes.

RHYTHM MODEL "C"

15

Note: In any *quarter*-note meter — such as $\frac{2}{4}$, $\frac{3}{4}$, $\frac{4}{4}$, etc. — the division of the 8th into two 16ths creates these traditional rhythm patterns:

1 - and-uh   1 - ee - and   1 - ee ___ uh   **Track 6** *Dictation*

Track 7

D You already know . . . that a half note is twice the length of a quarter note, and that a quarter note is twice the length of an 8th note.

New information: We can use notes of double duration in *any* meter. In any 8th-note meter, for example, a quarter note may replace two 8th notes.

RHYTHM MODEL "D"

Track 8 *Dictation*

Track 9

E You already know . . . that a dot after a note means "plus one-half."

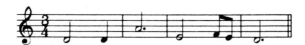

New information: We can apply this concept to *any* note value. A dot after a *quarter* note adds an extra *8th* to its length:

RHYTHM MODEL "E"

Track 10 *Dictation*

Track 11

F You now know . . . that the duration of the dotted quarter is equivalent to three 8th notes.

And you already know . . . that a tie ties together notes of the same pitch, making a longer sound.

New information: When a quarter note in one beat is tied to an 8th note in the next beat, the tied notes may be replaced by a *dotted quarter note.*

RHYTHM MODEL "F-1"

RHYTHM MODEL "F-2"

RHYTHM MODEL "F-3"

New information: A tied 8th-16th may often be replaced by a *dotted 8th note.* The dot after the 8th adds an extra *16th* to its length: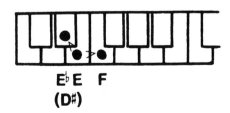

Track 12 *Dictation*

Track 13

MELODIC INTERVALS and MELODIC DICTATION

THE INTERVAL
The word *interval* means "space between." A musical interval is the distance separating any two tones, specifying how much higher or lower the two pitches are *relative to one another.*

HOW TO MEASURE AN INTERVAL
The exact distance between two pitches is calculated by using a standard unit of measure called the *half-step* or *semitone.* On the keyboard, a half-step is the distance between any key and its closest neighboring key. Neighbors may be black or white keys, either higher or lower.

17

THE CHROMATIC SCALE

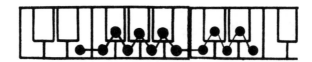

Although this example begins and ends on E, a chromatic scale may begin on *any* pitch, provided it follows this pattern of continuous half-steps.

MELODIC AND HARMONIC INTERVALS
A *melodic* interval is one in which the two pitches are played one after the other. A *harmonic* interval is one in which the two pitches are played at the same time.

MELODY AND HARMONY
The words *melody* and *melodic* refer to a group of *consecutive* pitches. The words *harmony* and *harmonic* refer to a group of *simultaneous* pitches.

"ENHARMONIC"

The term *enharmonic* describes two tones that sound exactly the same, but are named and written differently — such as E♭ and D♯.

TWO WAYS TO WRITE THE SAME HALF-STEP Track 14

(a) as a **chromatic half-step**:  (b) as a **minor 2nd**:

F - F♯   F - G♭

Minor and Major Seconds

THE MINOR SECOND: Three Distinctive Features
1. The letter names of the two pitches are in alphabetical order.
2. The two pitches are immediate neighbors on the staff: one is in a space, the other on the neighboring line.
3. The two pitches are a half-step apart on the keyboard.

THE MINOR SECOND ON THE KEYBOARD

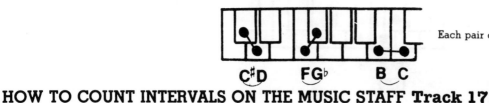

C♯D   FG♭   B C

Each pair of pitches is *one half-step* apart.

Track 15 *Dictation*

Track 16 *Dictation*

HOW TO COUNT INTERVALS ON THE MUSIC STAFF Track 17
Count the first note of the interval as "One." Then count up or down the staff (depending on which way the interval is going), from line to space to line, etc., until you reach the second note of the interval.

The number of the interval is the same as the number of moves you made on the staff to reach the second note.

TWO PARTS OF AN INTERVAL'S NAME

The *number* of the interval (such as "2nd") matches the line-space distance between the two pitches on the staff. The *tonal quality* of the interval — that is, its unique sound — is indicated by such words as "minor" and "major." The *complete* name of a specific interval then becomes "minor 2nd," "major 3rd," and so on.

THE MAJOR SECOND: Three Distinctive Features

1. The letter names of the two pitches are in alphabetical order.
2. The two pitches are immediate neighbors on the staff: one is in a space, the other on the neighboring line.
3. The two pitches are *two* half-steps (or *one whole-step*) apart on the keyboard.

THE MAJOR SECOND ON THE STAFF

THE MAJOR SECOND ON THE KEYBOARD

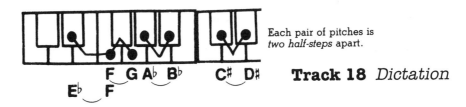

Each pair of pitches is *two half-steps* apart.

Track 18 *Dictation*

SIDE BY SIDE: Combinations of Minor and Major Seconds **Track 19**

A sample dictation combining minor and major seconds

A note about accidentals: Once you write an accidental in front of a note — a sharp, a flat, or a natural — that accidental holds good for the *entire* bar. In the example above, the *flat* before the first note (E) also affects the third note (E); *both* are played as E♭.

A *natural* is placed in front of a note in order to cancel a previous accidental in the same bar. In the example above, the natural before the fourth note (D) cancels the previous flat before the second note (D).

RHYTHM MODEL: for Melodic Dictation No. 13 **Track 20**

RHYTHM MODEL: for Melodic Dictation No. 14

19

RHYTHM MODEL: for Melodic Dictation No. 15

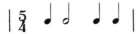

RHYTHM MODEL: for Melodic Dictation No. 16

RHYTHM MODEL: for Melodic Dictation No. 17

RHYTHM MODEL: for Melodic Dictation No. 18

A QUIZ ABOUT MINOR AND MAJOR SECONDS

1. What does **interval** mean?
2. In music, what standardized unit of measure do we use to calculate intervals?
3. What is a **half-step** or **semitone**?
4. What is a **chromatic scale**?
5. What is the difference between a **melodic** interval and a **harmonic** interval?
6. What does the term **enharmonic** mean?
7. What is the difference between a **chromatic half-step** and a **minor 2nd**?
8. What are the three distinctive features of all **minor 2nds**?
9. What are the three distinctive features of all **major 2nds**?
10. What is the purpose of a natural sign in front of a pitch?

Minor and Major Thirds

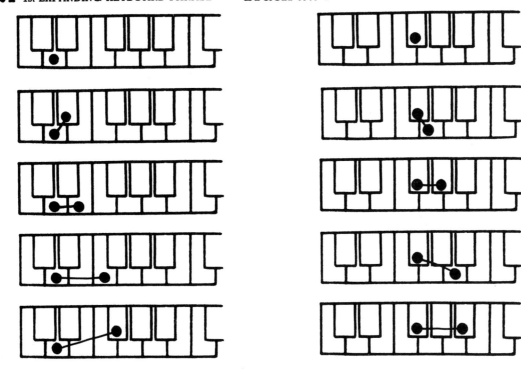

TRANSPOSITION Track 23

Transposition means the imitation of a melody or sequence of harmonies, using the same exact *pattern* as the original but moved to a different set of pitches.

THE MINOR THIRD AND THE MAJOR THIRD ON THE KEYBOARD Track 24

Minor 3rd   Major 3rd

MINOR AND MAJOR THIRDS ON THE STAFF

Minor 3rds   Major 3rds

F - Ab   C - Eb   C♯ - A♯   Bb - G   F - A   C - E   C♯ - A   Bb - Gb

Each pair of pitches is   Each pair of pitches is
three half-steps apart.   *four half-steps* (two whole-steps) apart.

DISTINCTIVE FEATURES OF *ALL* THIRDS

1. The two pitches of the interval are either in *two adjacent spaces* or on *two adjacent lines* of the staff.
2. The letter names of the two pitches *skip one letter* of the alphabet.
3. For the *minor* 3rd, the two pitches are *three* half-steps apart on the keyboard.
4. For the *major* 3rd, the two pitches are *four* half-steps (two whole-steps) apart on the keyboard.

A sample dictation combining minor and major thirds

RHYTHM MODEL: for Melodic Dictation No. 19 **Track 25**

RHYTHM MODEL: for Melodic Dictation No. 20

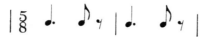

RHYTHM MODEL: for Melodic Dictation No. 21

RHYTHM MODEL: for Melodic Dictation No. 22

BRAHMS: Symphony No. 3 (3rd Movement; original notation)

The "pickup" bar: A piece of music may begin with an incomplete bar leading directly into the first downbeat of the music. This small preparation for the downbeat has the same feeling and function as a breath *in* before a breath *out,* or as the preparatory backswing of a golf club, racquet, or bat that precedes the forward motion to meet the ball. The "missing" part of the pickup bar is traditionally found in the *last* bar of the music, which is shortened to balance the number of beats in the pickup.

The pattern ♪. ♫ : The dot after the 16th note lengthens the 16th by one-half of its value: ♪ + ♪ = ♪.

The figure sounds the same as the tied notation

THE BRAHMS THEME, REWRITTEN IN 3/4 **Track 26**

RHYTHM MODEL: for Melodic Dictations Nos. 23-27

INTERVALS OF THE BRAHMS THEME

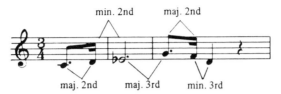

Track 27 *Dictation*

CD 3

The Perfect Fourth and the Perfect Fifth

INTERVAL LABELS Track 1

Seconds, 3rds, 6ths, and 7ths can be labeled *minor, major, augmented,* and *diminished* — such as the "minor 2nd," "augmented 2nd," "major 3rd," "minor 6th," and "diminished 7th."

The remaining intervals — the unison and octave, 4ths, and 5ths — can be labeled *perfect, augmented,* and *diminished.* They are never referred to as *major* or *minor.*

THE PERFECT FOURTH ON THE KEYBOARD

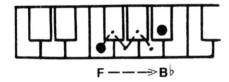

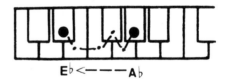

THE PERFECT FOURTH ON THE STAFF Track 2

Each pair of pitches
is *five half-steps* apart.

THE PERFECT FIFTH ON THE KEYBOARD Track 3

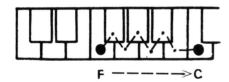

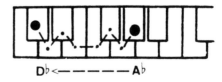

THE PERFECT FIFTH ON THE STAFF Track 4

Each pair of pitches
is *seven half-steps* apart.

SIDE BY SIDE: Combinations of Perfect Fourths and Fifths **Track 5**

A sample dictation combining perfect fourths and fifths

RHYTHM MODEL: for Melodic Dictation No. 30

RHYTHM MODEL: for Melodic Dictation No. 31

RHYTHM MODEL: for Melodic Dictation No. 32

RHYTHM MODEL: for Melodic Dictation No. 33

"SCARBOROUGH FAIR": A Model for Transposition **Track 6**

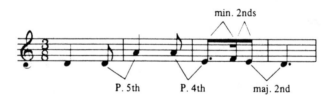

RHYTHM MODEL: for Melodic Dictations Nos. 34-40 **Track 7**

The Augmented Fourth and the Diminished Fifth Track 8

THE AUGMENTED FOURTH/DIMINISHED FIFTH ON THE KEYBOARD

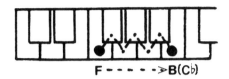 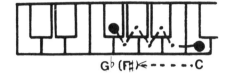

THE AUGMENTED FOURTH AND THE DIMINISHED FIFTH ON THE STAFF Track 9

EXPANDING THE PERFECT 4th

 or

CONTRACTING THE PERFECT 5th

 or

DOUBLE FLATS AND DOUBLE SHARPS

A flatted note can be *lowered* by one half-step by writing the accidental ♭♭ (double flat) in front of the note. A sharped note can be *raised* by one half-step by writing the accidental x (double sharp) in front of the note. Although any double-flatted or double-sharped note can be written enharmonically as a "white" key (B♭♭ = A; Fx = G), the use of the double accidental allows the writer to retain both the letter name and staff position (line or space) or the original note, thus keeping the identity of the interval intact.

CHOPIN: Etude in E♭ Minor, Op.10, No.6 Track 10

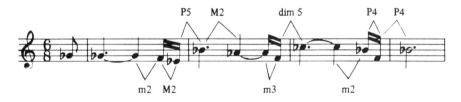

Note: This analysis uses simplified interval labels: "m" for *minor*, "M" for *major*, and "P" for *perfect*. The labels "dim" and "aug" are as usual, without periods. An interval *number* may be written as shown: "2" and "5" instead of "2nd" and "5th," etc.

RHYTHM MODEL: for Melodic Dictations Nos. 41-43 Track 11

RHYTHM MODEL: for Melodic Dictations Nos. 44-47 Track 12

RHYTHM MODEL: for Melodic Dictation No. 48

Track 13

The Minor Sixth and the Major Sixth

THE MINOR SIXTH ON THE KEYBOARD

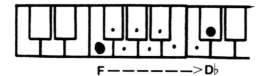

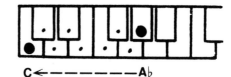

THE MAJOR SIXTH ON THE KEYBOARD

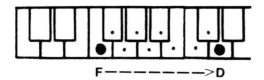

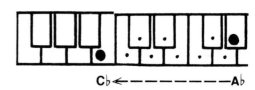

MINOR AND MAJOR SIXTHS ON THE STAFF Track 14

Minor 6ths

Each pair of pitches is *eight* half-steps
(four whole-steps) apart.

Major 6ths

Each pair of pitches is *nine* half-steps
(four-and-a-half steps) apart.

MOZART: Piano Concerto No. 21 (slow movement) **Track 15**

*The symbol C is a traditional substitute for $\frac{4}{4}$.

26

Note: How to Count the Double Dot

A *single* dot after a note means "plus one-half":

The *second* dot adds an extra length to the note value equivalent to *one-half of the value of the first dot:*

(1st (2nd
dot) dot)

Renotated as *tied* notes, the Mozart theme would look like this . . .

. . . or, more simply (with exactly the same sound), like this:

INTERVALS OF THE MOZART THEME

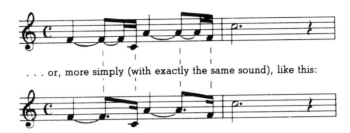

RHYTHM MODEL: for Melodic Dictations Nos. 49-61 Track 16, 17, 18, 19

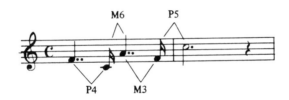

(There are no rhythm models for Melodic Dictations Nos. 62-64.)

CD 4

Track 1   Track 2

Combined Dictations Nos. 1-17, requiring solutions to both the rhythm pattern and intervals of each example.

"THE HARMONIOUS TRIO" Track 3

Harmonic Intervals, Harmonic Dictation, and the Triad

THE TRIAD

A *triad* is a harmonious trio of pitches, made of any starting pitch, with any kind of 3rd added above it, and then with any kind of 5th added above it.

27

PLAYING HARMONIC INTERVALS

The Minor 3rd on the Keyboard

The Major 3rd on the Keyboard

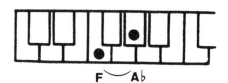

"ROOT"

The label *root* refers to the starting, or fundamental, pitch on which any chord is built.

MINOR AND MAJOR THIRDS
WRITTEN AS HARMONIC INTERVALS ON THE STAFF Track 4

PLAYING MORE HARMONIC INTERVALS Track 5

The Diminished 5th
on the Keyboard

The Perfect 5th
on the Keyboard

The Augmented 5th
on the Keyboard

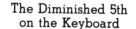
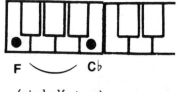

(*six* half-steps)

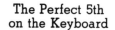
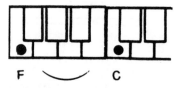

(*seven* half-steps)

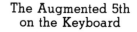
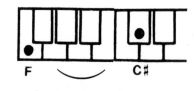

(*eight* half-steps)

THE AUGMENTED FIFTH

The *augmented 5th* is one half-step larger than the perfect 5th. It consists of eight half-steps (or four whole-steps) between its two pitches. The *sound* of the augmented 5th is identical to the sound of the minor 6th — that is, the two intervals are *enharmonic* versions of the same sound:

RHYTHM MODEL: for Harmonic Dictations Nos. 1-5 Track 6

RHYTHM MODEL: for Harmonic Dictations Nos. 6-10 Track 7

THE MAJOR TRIAD Track 8

The *major triad* consists of a root, a *major* 3rd above the root, and a *perfect* 5th above the root.

The major triad on the keyboard . . . . and on the staff

28

THE MINOR TRIAD

The *minor triad* consists of a root, a *minor* 3rd above the root, and a *perfect* 5th above the root.

The minor triad on the keyboard . . . .   and on the staff

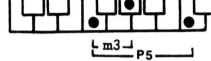

CHORD SYMBOLS: Major and Minor Triads

Major triad: Use only the letter name of the root (F, E♭, C#, etc.)
Minor triad: Use the letter name of the root, followed by *m* (Fm, E♭m, C#m, etc.).

MAJOR AND MINOR TRIADS ON THE STAFF, WITH THEIR CHORD SYMBOLS

RHYTHM MODEL: for Harmonic Dictations Nos. 11-14 Track 9

THE DIMINISHED TRIAD Track 10

The *diminished triad* consists of a root, a *minor* 3rd above the root, and a *diminished* 5th above the root.

The diminished triad on the keyboard . . . . and on the staff

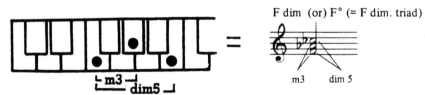

CHORD SYMBOLS: The Diminished Triad

To label a diminished triad, use the letter name of the root, followed either by *dim* or the tiny circle °
(F°, E♭°, C#dim, etc.). The two symbols mean the same thing.

MINOR AND DIMINISHED TRIADS ON THE STAFF, WITH THEIR CHORD SYMBOLS

RHYTHM MODEL: for Harmonic Dictations Nos. 15-18 Track 11

A SAMPLE DICTATION
COMBINING MAJOR, MINOR, AND DIMINISHED TRIADS Track 12

RHYTHM MODEL: for Harmonic Dictations Nos. 19-22

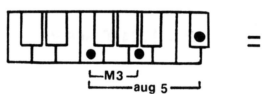

THE AUGMENTED TRIAD Track 13

The *augmented triad* consists of a root, a *major* 3rd above the root, and an *augmented* 5th above the root.

The augmented triad on the keyboard . . . .   and on the staff

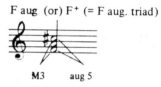

CHORD SYMBOLS: The Augmented Triad

To label an augmented triad, use the letter name of the root, followed either by *aug* or a small "plus" sign + (Faug, Eb +, C# +, etc.). The two symbols mean the same thing.

MAJOR AND AUGMENTED TRIADS ON THE STAFF, WITH THEIR CHORD SYMBOLS

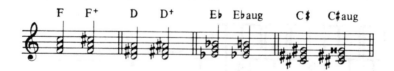

A SAMPLE DICTATION
COMBINING MAJOR, MINOR, AND AUGMENTED TRIADS Track 14

Note: To write a dotted note on a staff *line*, place the dot *above* the line, in the neighboring space:

RHYTHM MODEL: for Harmonic Dictations Nos. 23-26

A SAMPLE DICTATION COMBINING FOUR KINDS OF TRIADS

RHYTHM MODEL: for Harmonic Dictations Nos. 27-30 Track 15

THE FOUR TRIADS AT A GLANCE

name	Major Triad	Minor Triad	Diminished Triad	Augmented Triad
chord symbol	F, E♭, C# (etc.)	Fm, E♭ m, C#m (etc.)	F° or Fdim, E♭ ° or E dim, C#° or C#dim (etc.)	F + or Faug, E♭ + or E aug, C# + or C#aug. (etc.)
kind of 5th	P5	P5	dim5	aug5
kind of 3rd	M3	m3	m3	M3
starting pitch	root	root	root	root

Note: Each triad can also be analyzed as a *pair* of 3rds, one above the other:

Major Triad

Minor Triad

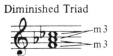

Diminished Triad

Augmented Triad

CD 5

INTERVALS AND CHORDS OF THE SEVENTH Track 1
The Major and the Minor Seventh

MAJOR AND MINOR SEVENTHS ON THE KEYBOARD

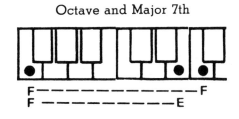

Octave and Major 7th

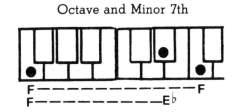

Octave and Minor 7th

31

MAJOR AND MINOR SEVENTHS ON THE STAFF Track 2

The Major 7th (melodic and harmonic notation)

Each pair of pitches is *one half-step* smaller than the octave.

The Minor 7th (melodic and harmonic notation)

Each pair of pitches is *two half-steps* (one whole-step) smaller than the octave.

"A SENTIMENTAL WALTZ" (Part 1) Track 3

The slur: The curved line ⌒ unites notes with *different* pitches, telling the performer to play all of the notes under the slur as smoothly as possible.

INTERVALS OF THE WALTZ (Part 1) Track 4

A SAMPLE TRANSPOSITION OF THE WALTZ (Part 1)

RHYTHM MODEL: for Waltz Transpositions Nos. 1-4 Track 5

"A SENTIMENTAL WALTZ" (Part 2) Track 6

INTERVALS OF THE WALTZ (Part 2)

A SAMPLE TRANSPOSITION OF THE WALTZ (Part 2)

RHYTHM MODEL: for Waltz Transpositions Nos. 5-8 Track 7

A SAMPLE REARRANGEMENT OF THE WALTZ PHRASES Track 8

RHYTHM MODEL: for Waltz Transpositions Nos. 9-12

"THE HARMONIOUS QUARTET"
Seventh Chords

THE BRIDGE FROM MELODY TO HARMONY Track 9

"A SENTIMENTAL WALTZ" (Part 1): Phrases 1 & 2

THE TRIAD AND THE MAJOR SEVENTH CHORD
ON THE STAFF, WITH THEIR CHORD SYMBOLS

THE MAJOR TRIAD WITH A DOUBLED ROOT

In the example above, the first chord of each pair of chords is a *major* triad. The addition of the extra root — the top note of the harmony — simply thickens the chordal sound without changing the identity of the chord as a triad.

THE MAJOR SEVENTH CHORD

The *major 7th chord* consists of a root, *major* 3rd, *perfect* 5th and *major* 7th.

The chord symbol for the major 7th chord consists of two elements: first, the letter name of the root (F, D, E♭ , C#, etc.), indicating that the chord is *based on a major triad;* and, second, the symbol *maj 7,* telling us that the chord contains the interval of a major 7th above the root (F^maj7, D^maj 7, E♭ ^maj 7, C#^maj 7, etc.).

"A SENTIMENTAL WALTZ (Part 1): Phrase 3

THE MAJOR SEVENTH CHORD AND THE DOMINANT SEVENTH
ON THE STAFF, WITH THEIR CHORD SYMBOLS

THE DOMINANT SEVENTH

The *dominant 7th* consists of a root, *major* 3rd, *perfect* 5th, and *minor* 7th.

The chord symbol for the dominant 7th consists of two elements: first, the letter name of the root (F, D, E♭ , C#, etc.), indicating that the chord is *based on a major triad;* and, second, the symbol *7,* telling us that the chord contains the interval of a minor 7th above the root (F^7, D^7, E♭ ^7, C#^7, etc.). (In chord symbols, the plain number *7* always indicates a *minor* 7th above the root of the chord. The symbol "min 7" does not exist.)

THE MAJOR TRIAD, MAJOR SEVENTH CHORD, AND DOMINANT SEVENTH

Note that in each trio of chords, the root, 3rd, and 5th are identical. Only the top note changes, moving by half-steps downward from the octave.

SEVENTH CHORDS ON THE STAFF

When any 7th chord is notated in its simplest, basic voicing (as in the example above) of root, 3rd, 5th, and 7th, all four pitches of the chord will be either space notes *or* line notes.

A SAMPLE DICTATION
COMBINING THE TRIAD, THE MAJOR SEVENTH CHORD, AND THE DOMINANT SEVENTH

RHYTHM MODEL: for Harmonic Dictations Nos. 31-34 **Track 10**

THE BRIDGE FROM MELODY TO HARMONY (Minor Version) **Track 11**

THE TRIAD AND THE MINOR/MAJOR SEVENTH
ON THE STAFF, WITH THEIR CHORD SYMBOLS

THE MINOR TRIAD WITH A DOUBLED ROOT

In the example above, the first chord of each pair of chords is a *minor* triad. The addition of the extra root — the top note of the harmony — simply thickens the chordal sound without changing the identity of the chord as a triad.

THE MINOR/MAJOR SEVENTH

The *minor/major 7th chord* consists of a root, *minor* 3rd, *perfect* 5th, and *major* 7th.
The chord symbol for the minor/major 7th consists of two elements: first, the letter name of the root, followed by *m* (Fm, Dm, E♭ m, C#m, etc.), indicating that the chord is *based on a minor triad;* and, second, the symbol *maj.7,* telling us that the chord contains the interval of a major 7th above the root (Fm$^{maj.7}$, Dm$^{maj.7}$, E♭ m$^{maj.7}$, C#m$^{maj.7}$, etc.).

"A SENTIMENTAL WALTZ" (Part 2): Phrase 3

THE MINOR/MAJOR SEVENTH AND THE MINOR SEVENTH
ON THE STAFF, WITH THEIR CHORD SYMBOLS

THE MINOR SEVENTH CHORD

The *minor 7th chord* consists of a root, *minor* 3rd, *perfect* 5th, and *minor* 7th.

The chord symbol for the minor 7th chord consists of two elements: first, the letter name of the root, followed by *m* (Fm, Dm, E♭ m, C#m, etc.), indicating that the chord is *based on a minor triad;* and, second, the symbol *7,* telling us that the chord contains the interval of a minor 7th above the root (Fm⁷, Dm⁷, E♭ m⁷, C#m⁷, etc.).

THE MINOR TRIAD, MINOR/MAJOR SEVENTH, AND MINOR SEVENTH

Note that in each trio of chords, the root, 3rd, and 5th are identical. Only the top note changes, moving by half-steps downward from the octave.

A SAMPLE DICTATION COMBINING THE MINOR TRIAD,
THE MINOR/MAJOR SEVENTH, AND THE MINOR SEVENTH

RHYTHM MODEL: for Harmonic Dictations Nos. 35-40 **Track 12**

VARIOUS SEVENTH-CHORD PROGRESSIONS
(A Sampling of Additional Combinations for Further Study)

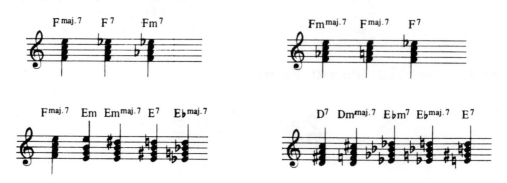

36

Solutions to the Rhythmic Dictation Exercises

CD 1 / Track 7, 9, 11

CD 1 / Track 13, 23

CD 1 / Track 27, 31, 33

CD 2 / Track 2, 6, 8, 10, 12

Solutions to the Melodic Dictation Exercises

CD 2 / Track 15, 16, 18, 20

CD 2 / Track 25, 26, 27

CD 3 / Track 5, 7

CD 3 / Track 11, 12

CD 3 / Track 16, 17, 18

Solutions to the Combined Dictation Exercises

CD 4 / Track 1, 2

41

Solutions to the Harmonic Dictation Exercises

CD 4 / Track 6, 7, 8

CD 4 / Track 9, 11, 12, 14, 15

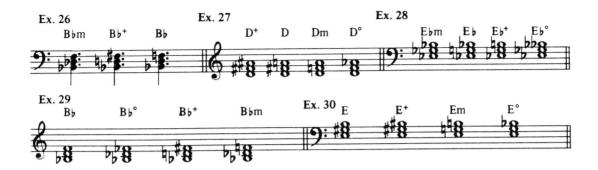

Solutions to the Waltz Transposition Dictations

CD 5 / Track 5, 7, 8

Solutions to the Harmonic Dictation Exercises (cont'd)

CD 5 / Track 10, 12